WW3 Isn't What You Thought It Would Be

The Silent War of the 21st Century

By Nicholas Salerno III

WW3 Isn't What You Thought It Would Be

Nicholas Salerno III

Published by Nicholas Salerno III, 2023.

WW3 ISN'T WHAT YOU THOUGHT IT WOULD BE

First edition. September 16, 2023.

ISBN: 979-8223772200

Written by Nicholas Salerno III.

Table of Contents

Dedicated to the souls who have been claimed by global tragedies and the resilient hearts left behind to remember them.

Legal Disclaimer

The information, views, and opinions expressed in this book are those of the author and do not necessarily reflect the views, opinions, or official policies of any other individual, organization, company, or government entity. The book is provided for informational and entertainment purposes only.

While every attempt has been made to verify the information provided in this publication, neither the author nor the publisher assumes any responsibility for errors, omissions, or contrary interpretations of the subject matter herein.

This book is not intended as a substitute for professional advice or counsel. Readers are advised to seek the services of competent professionals in legal, business, financial, health, or other specialized fields before acting upon any information in this book.

Neither the author nor the publisher is responsible for any actions taken, results, losses, damages, or distress caused, either directly or indirectly, from information provided in this book or from any accompanying or related material.

All readers are encouraged to use their judgment and discretion when interpreting and using the information provided in this book.

Introduction

A Word from the Author

As I sat at my desk, engrossed in the bewildering events surrounding the recent Maui fire, I couldn't help but revisit my research from years past. It was like a treasure chest of unanswered questions and unsettling truths. I came to a startling realization: we are living through a hidden war, one so disguised and intricate that most of us don't even realize it's happening.

The story began with the fires that have consumed vast landscapes and lives, from Paradise, California, to the heart of Maui. We were told these were "natural disasters," calamities beyond human control. Yet, a plethora of questions remained unanswered. Why locals were told the Maui fire was 100% contained? Why was there no warning siren? Why water supplies were mysteriously cut off? The inconsistencies led me down a rabbit hole of deception, control, and the question of who benefits from such disasters.

What I found was a staggering labyrinth of interests, from governmental bodies to corporations and billionaires. These powerful entities have harnessed disasters, misinformation, and technological advances for their gain, leaving the rest of us in the dark—or worse, in a state of ruin.

This book is not merely an expose or a catalogue of theories; it is a call to action. You will explore the stark realities of our world today: from the illusion of global warming to the cunning guise of unbiased news, from the exploitation of natural disasters to the weaponization of modern technologies like 5G and RNA manipulation in vaccines.

My journey through the heart of Maui's fires, along with my prior research, has left me with no option but to break my silence. It is my sincere hope that by the end of this book, you too will question, you too will doubt, and you too will realize the magnitude of the hidden war that is taking place all around us.

Chapter 1

Global Warming: A Deceptive Mirage

We've been told for years that global warming is the existential threat of our age. Sweeping climate policies have been initiated, and trillions are being spent to mitigate a catastrophe. But what if I told you that this picture isn't as clear-cut as it seems?

The notion that the Earth is warming is based on a set of data points, often selectively chosen, that serve a narrative beneficial to certain groups. And yet, Earth's climate is incredibly complex. It's influenced by the tilt of our planet's axis, ocean currents, and even volcanic activity, among other factors. Moreover, the sun doesn't warm the Earth uniformly. Different regions receive sunlight at various angles, and it's preposterous to attribute a single, linear cause to a multifaceted issue.

Consider this: in the early 1970s, scientists were warning us about global cooling, predicting a new ice age. Those claims were as vehement as today's warnings about global warming. The question that looms large is, why the shift in narrative?

Investigating deeper, you'll find that large corporations have invested heavily in renewable energy projects, set to profit enormously from the transition away from fossil fuels. It's a neat package: create a crisis and offer the solution, reaping benefits on both ends.

So, what about the opposing voices in the scientific community? Many have been systematically silenced or discredited. Their grants are pulled, their papers rejected, their characters maligned. The goal is to have a monolithic voice that serves a particular agenda.

The 'Green Movement' isn't as altruistic as it appears. From carbon trading to green technology patents, there's big money involved. Even the most well-intentioned environmental activists may be pawns in a larger game they don't fully comprehend.

Then there's the issue of manipulated data. Temperature records have been adjusted to fit the narrative. And let's not forget the 'Climategate' scandal of 2009, where leaked emails from climate scientists indicated potential conspiracies to distort research findings.

If global warming were a settled science, why would there be any need to manipulate data or silence opposition? Isn't the hallmark of scientific integrity the openness to challenge and validation?

One of the most glaring examples of this narrative manipulation is the Paris Agreement. It promises to keep global temperatures from rising 2°C above pre-industrial levels. But dig deeper, and you'll find that the most significant emitters like China are given a free pass until 2030. Meanwhile, developed nations are financially burdened, contributing to a significant wealth transfer from West to East.

It's high time we start questioning the mainstream narrative surrounding global warming. It's not about denying the importance of caring for our planet; it's about seeking the truth behind the veil of misinformation. In an era where disaster capitalism reigns supreme, and natural calamities serve as opportunities for societal overhaul, we owe it to ourselves to be the watchdogs of our destiny.

Further Reading:

- "The Great Global Warming Swindle" – Documentary
- "State of Fear" by Michael Crichton
- "Climategate: The CRUtape Letters" by Steven Mosher and Thomas Fuller

Chapter 2

The New Warfront: Disasters and Government Takeovers

When you think of war, images of battlefields, tanks, and soldiers come to mind. But what if war has evolved to a point where no shots need to be fired, and the battlefields are our very communities? The Paradise Camp Fire in California is a chilling example of this new form of warfare, and its ramifications go beyond the loss of life and property.

This devastating fire didn't just cause destruction; it also set the stage for government intervention in the electricity sector. The fire's origins were traced back to malfunctioning equipment owned by Pacific Gas and Electric (PG&E), which led to its bankruptcy and a subsequent government takeover. This is a classic example of the disaster capitalism model, wherein a catastrophe creates an opportunity for government or big corporations to seize control of essential resources and services. In essence, the fire facilitated a monopoly over California's electricity supply, making every citizen dependent on a government-run utility.

But why did the fire burn so hot? Soil tests in the area showed unusually high levels of aluminum. While aluminum is naturally occurring, the elevated levels led some to point fingers at "cloud seeding" or "chemtrails" as a possible culprit. Whether or not cloud seeding played a role, the presence of aluminum could have intensified the fire, making it burn hotter and faster, further enabling the disaster capitalism model.

This isn't a dystopian fiction; this is a reality unfolding in front of us. Like a boa constrictor slowly squeezing its prey, this new form of warfare tightens its grip subtly, making it difficult to point to a single enemy or action that catalyzed it all.

It's worth noting that a government-run electricity monopoly isn't intrinsically bad. However, when it emerges from a disaster that was potentially preventable or even artificially exacerbated, questions about motives become unavoidable. And the Paradise Camp Fire isn't an isolated event. It's a cog in a machine that seems to be setting the stage for what some refer to as "The Great Reset," a restructuring of societal norms and control mechanisms.

We need to be vigilant. We need to ask questions, probe the events surrounding these disasters, and examine who benefits in the aftermath. The stakes are too high to accept the official narratives blindly. Our future, our freedom, and our ability to govern ourselves are on the line.

Further Reading:

- "The Shock Doctrine" by Naomi Klein
- "Disaster Capitalism: Making a Killing out of Catastrophe" by Antony Loewenstein
- "The Uninhabitable Earth: Life After Warming" by David Wallace-Wells

Chapter 3

The Manipulated Media - A Battle for Truth

In a world filled with data, the power to filter and disseminate information is perhaps one of the greatest powers anyone can hold. With the media landscape majorly controlled by a handful of corporations, the potential for biased news is at an all-time high. You may have heard that most media outlets in the United States are owned by just three major corporations: Comcast, Disney, and AT&T. The consolidation of media under a few giants puts objectivity at risk and makes it a perfect platform to feed the disaster capitalism model we discussed earlier.

The implications of this are far-reaching and tie back to every other issue we've discussed so far. Whether it's the narrative surrounding disasters, government interventions, or even ongoing health crises, the lack of diverse viewpoints and independent journalism undermines the principles of a democratic society. Information, whether true or manipulated, shapes public opinion and thus guides public action or inaction.

Take, for example, the coverage of the Paradise Camp Fire and the subsequent government takeover of the electric company. How much of the coverage dug into the questionable aspects of the fire, like the aluminum content in the soil? How many reports questioned the swift government intervention and what that means for the future of public utilities?

This isn't just about media's role in the United States; it's a global issue that affects how crises, both natural and man-made, are managed and how the 'victors' are decided in this silent war. If we are to protect our liberties and maintain a society where power is held by the people, media reform isn't just an option—it's a necessity.

The media's role in this new warfare is as pivotal as any weapon system. It shapes perceptions, influences decisions, and can tip the balance between freedom and control. Media literacy, diversity in news sources, and active civic participation are not just lofty ideals but essential practices if we hope to counter this monolithic narrative machine.

Further Reading:

- "Manufacturing Consent" by Edward S. Herman and Noam Chomsky
- "Trust Me, I'm Lying" by Ryan Holiday
- "The Filter Bubble" by Eli Pariser

Chapter 4

Toxic Elements - Silver Iodide, Fluoride, and the War Under Our Feet

The silent war isn't only being fought in the airwaves and digital screens; it's happening right beneath our feet. From the soil we cultivate to the water we drink, the elements that sustain life are being tampered with in ways that support a disaster capitalism model and serve a few powerful entities.

One lesser-known but significant aspect is cloud seeding using silver iodide. The intention is often benign—increasing rainfall for agriculture or controlling forest fires. However, the introduction of silver iodide into the environment has its own set of consequences, such as toxicity in aquatic life and soil contamination. It raises an important question: Are we solving one problem while creating another?

Fluoride is another contentious element, especially in the U.S., where it is added to public drinking water ostensibly to improve dental health. Yet, concerns persist about its potential negative effects, including neurotoxicity and endocrine disruption. This goes beyond individual health; it's a matter of public agency. Should government entities have the right to add substances to public resources?

This issue goes back to the land, as well. The presence of aluminum in the soil, as was found after the Paradise Camp Fire, hints at yet another layer of environmental manipulation. Aluminum is highly reactive and can exacerbate fires, among other ecological disruptions.

Understanding what's in our soil, water, and even our air isn't just an environmental issue; it's a civil liberties issue. It ties back to the core idea of control in this silent war—control over resources, control over health, and ultimately, control over populations.

Further Reading:

- "Our Stolen Future" by Theo Colborn, Dianne Dumanoski, and John Peterson Myers
- "Silent Spring" by Rachel Carson
- "The Fluoride Deception" by Christopher Bryson

In our battle for truth and freedom, the environment under our feet and the water we drink are as much battlefields as any other platform. They are realms where the silent war manifests in subtle yet impactful ways, urging us to look down and question what we've always taken for granted.

Chapter 5

The Unseen War - Drugs, Homelessness, and Social Disintegration

In our quest for truth and freedom, we must not overlook the social crises that are both a cause and consequence of this silent war. Walk through any city, and you'll encounter an aspect of the conflict that doesn't require a conspiracy theory to explain: the growing epidemic of drug addiction and homelessness.

Many see these as isolated social issues, but they are not. They are woven into the very fabric of a silent war that exploits human vulnerability for profit and social control. These are your fellow humans, your neighbors, who, like soldiers on a battlefield, have been left scarred, often forgotten by the systems that should care for them.

In recent years, the opioid crisis has claimed lives in numbers exceeding those of some conventional wars. Yet, the war on drugs seems to be a war on the people, selectively enforced to deepen social divides and disproportionately affect marginalized communities.

It's hard to ignore the irony. The nation that was founded on the ideals of freedom and individual liberties now hosts a booming private prison industry, a consequence of strict drug laws. The "land of the free" has the highest incarceration rate globally, much of it drug-related. Our forefathers fought the Revolutionary War for freedom; what would they say about this?

Homelessness, too, has its roots in systemic issues. Housing-first policies work but are often rejected in favor of more punitive measures that make it a crime to be homeless. Imagine if your dearest loved ones were caught in this trap, exploited by a system geared toward profit rather than social welfare.

Further Reading:

- "Dreamland: The True Tale of America's Opiate Epidemic" by Sam Quinones
- "Evicted: Poverty and Profit in the American City" by Matthew Desmond
- "The New Jim Crow: Mass Incarceration in the Age of Colorblindness" by Michelle Alexander

As we delve deeper into this crisis, it becomes clear that compassion, love, and systemic change are the ways forward. Love, after all, was the driving force behind the Revolutionary War; love for freedom, for self-determination, and for the potential of a better future.

Chapter 6

Disaster Capitalism: Exploiting Chaos

In the annals of modern history, moments of great turmoil, be they natural or man-made, have been seen as moments of introspection, of unity. However, not all see them this way. For some, disasters are not events to be mitigated but rather opportunities to be exploited. Enter the arena of "disaster capitalism," a term popularized by journalist Naomi Klein in her seminal work "The Shock Doctrine." It refers to the practice of governments and private entities capitalizing on collective shocks created by disasters to push through radical policies that enrich a small elite at the expense of the masses.

Flames of Opportunity

The tragic Paradise Camp Fire, the wildfires that ravaged Maui, and many others globally stand testament to the devastating effects of unchecked climatic events. But the burnt aftermath of such tragedies, for some, is fertile ground for opportunism. How does disaster capitalism manifest in the wake of wildfires?

After the embers cool, there's an immediate need for rebuilding. Private contractors, some with direct ties to those in power, are often awarded lucrative contracts for reconstruction, many times without transparency or public scrutiny. Land previously occupied by the less affluent may suddenly find itself in the crosshairs of luxury developers. An electric company's perceived negligence can pave the way for governments to consolidate power over utilities, sometimes leading to even less oversight than before.

The Misinformation Inferno

News, in its ideal form, is a beacon of truth, guiding society through the smoke of misinformation. Yet, in today's fragmented media landscape, truth is often the first casualty. When disasters strike, the first narratives, whether true or false, can shape public perception for years to come.

In the age of the 24-hour news cycle, there's a race not just to be accurate, but to be first. In this rush, mistakes are made, narratives are spun, and those who can gain from misinformation stand ready to stoke the flames. When most media outlets are controlled by a handful of moguls, the narrative can be easily manipulated to serve vested interests. What's reported, how it's reported, and most importantly, what's omitted, can sculpt public opinion to favor policies and actions that feed into the disaster capitalism model.

Rebuilding or Reshaping?

Post-disaster scenarios offer the dual prospect of rebuilding and reshaping. The difference between the two is intent. Rebuilding seeks to restore and improve upon what existed before, while reshaping often serves a hidden agenda.

The Maui fire provides a compelling example. Discrepancies between grassroots accounts and official narratives, dubious decision-making during the crisis, and the contrasting treatment of tourists and locals hint at a deeper play. Was it sheer incompetence, or was it a part of a more extensive playbook of disaster capitalism?

Profits from Pain

At the heart of disaster capitalism lies an uncomfortable truth: there's immense profit in pain. From the reconstruction contracts post-disasters to land grabs, the potential for monetary gain is colossal. Even beyond immediate economic gains, there's the opportunity to usher in policy changes, deregulation, and privatization efforts that might have faced vehement opposition in more 'normal' times.

An Awakening

However, all is not bleak. The very fact that terms like "disaster capitalism" have entered the public lexicon suggests an awakening. Communities globally are becoming more vigilant, challenging official narratives, demanding transparency, and holding power to account. The fires, both literal and metaphorical, illuminate not just the shadows of opportunism but also the indomitable spirit of communities seeking truth and justice.

In a world that seems increasingly chaotic, it's essential to understand the undercurrents shaping our reality. By recognizing the patterns of disaster capitalism, society can strive to ensure that tragedies aren't compounded by exploitation.

Further Reading:

"The Shock Doctrine: The Rise of Disaster Capitalism" by Naomi Klein.

Chapter 7

Control through 5G "A Technological Weapon"

From the advent of fire to the invention of the wheel, technological progress has propelled humanity forward. However, with every breakthrough, there's an underbelly, a darker side that, if unchecked, can erode the very essence of human freedom and health. Today, that technological marvel, or for some, that monstrosity, is 5G.

The 5G Promise

5G, or fifth-generation technology, promises super-fast internet, a more connected world, and advancements in fields like virtual reality and telemedicine. Cities envision entire ecosystems built on 5G, enabling everything from smart traffic systems to advanced utility grids. With speeds up to 100 times faster than 4G, the leap is more than incremental—it's revolutionary. But at what cost?

The Health Implications: RF and EMF

Every wireless device emits radio frequencies (RF) and electromagnetic fields (EMF). While the science on the health impacts of 4G and earlier generations is still debated, 5G presents a more potent challenge. Given its frequency and the need for more base stations due to its shorter range, the exposure levels are set to increase exponentially.

There are several studies, albeit in their early stages, suggesting potential health risks associated with prolonged RF and EMF exposure. These range from sleep disturbances to more severe concerns like cancer. While definitive, large-scale studies on 5G are still pending, the surge in RF and EMF levels has made health experts and activists apprehensive.

A Weapon in Disguise?

Beyond health, 5G, with its ubiquitous connectivity, offers unparalleled surveillance capabilities. Imagine smart devices in homes, streets, and workplaces continuously connected, always watching, always listening. The data this generates is gold for marketers but also invaluable for surveillance states.

Coupled with AI, 5G could enable real-time monitoring on an unprecedented scale, making Orwell's "1984" seem less like fiction and more a forecast. This isn't just about governments spying on citizens; it's about control, influence, and manipulation. An omnipresent surveillance apparatus can curb dissent, manipulate public opinion, and even predict and pre-empt citizen actions.

Water, Vitamin D, and 5G

There's an under-researched area where 5G potentially impacts our health: its effects on water molecules and Vitamin D absorption. The human body is roughly 60% water. Some scientists believe that the frequencies used by 5G could resonate with water molecules, affecting their structure and thus, potentially our health. Moreover, there's speculation (though not widely accepted in the scientific community) that 5G could impact our skin's ability to produce Vitamin D, an essential nutrient.

Between Conspiracy and Caution

It's vital to tread a line between conspiracy theories and genuine concerns. Not every claim against 5G is grounded in science. However, the rush to deploy 5G networks worldwide with limited research on potential long-term health and societal impacts is a significant concern.

Conclusion: The Path Ahead

Technological progress is inevitable and, for the most part, desirable. But with something as pervasive as 5G, caution is paramount. It requires rigorous, transparent, and independent research into its potential effects on health and society. As consumers, it's crucial to stay informed, demand transparency from service providers, and push for regulations that prioritize public health over profits.

As 5G rolls out, the line between a connected utopia and a surveillance-driven dystopia blurs. It's up to individuals, communities, and governments to ensure that this technological leap doesn't come at the cost of our health, freedom, or democracy.

Further Reading:

1. "The Invisible Rainbow: A History of Electricity and Life" by Arthur Firstenberg.
2. "5G: Great risk for EU, U.S. and International Health! Compelling Evidence for Eight Distinct Types of Great Harm Caused by Electromagnetic Field (EMF) Exposures and the Mechanism that Causes Them" by Martin L. Pall.

Chapter 8

The COVID-19 Connection: RNA Manipulation and Control

In the annals of human history, few events have created such a seismic shift as the COVID-19 pandemic. Societies worldwide were locked down, economies ground to a halt, and our concept of "normal" was upended. As with any significant event, there's a tapestry of theories, speculation, and narratives—both mainstream and alternative. One of these theories connects 5G technology to the emergence and spread of COVID-19, weaving a tale of RNA manipulation, societal control, and a new world order.

5G and COVID-19: The Theory

The theory positing a connection between 5G and COVID-19 gained traction in some online circles. Proponents suggest that 5G radiation weakens the immune system, making people more susceptible to the virus. Some even claimed that the virus itself was a result of 5G radiation. These claims, it's essential to note, have been largely debunked by scientists, virologists, and telecommunication experts.

The Real Connection: A Control Narrative

While the direct link between 5G radiation and the virus is speculative, a different, less direct connection arises when one delves deeper into the societal changes both have engendered. The swift rollout of 5G and the equally rapid global spread of COVID-19 both enabled increased control over societies worldwide.

RNA Manipulation: The mRNA Vaccines

The introduction of mRNA vaccines, a first in vaccine history, brought both hope and skepticism. These vaccines use messenger RNA to instruct cells to produce a harmless piece of the virus, which in turn triggers an immune response. While this technology promises rapid vaccine development for future pathogens, it also brought forth concerns. The primary worry is the long-term effects of manipulating RNA—a critical molecule in our biology—and introducing it into billions of people.

From Health Crisis to Control Mechanism

With the pandemic came lockdowns, mask mandates, and, most importantly, a surge in surveillance. Contact tracing, movement mapping, and health status monitoring became integral tools in managing the pandemic. However, they also provided governments and institutions with an unparalleled peek into individual lives and behaviors.

Linking back to the previous chapter on 5G, the infrastructure for this enhanced surveillance was largely enabled by advanced communication technologies. While it wasn't necessarily the cause of the pandemic, 5G's rapid data transfer and connectivity became instrumental in the "pandemic response" narrative.

The Controlled Society

Lockdowns and surveillance birthed a controlled society—a society where movement was restricted, gatherings monitored, and dissent often silenced. This wasn't just a health measure; it was a social experiment on a global scale. For the first time, governments could gauge real-time responses to large-scale control measures.

As people were isolated, screens became the primary mode of connection, again reinforcing the role of technology in shaping narratives. With 5G set to increase this connectivity manifold, imagining a world of continuous real-time surveillance isn't far-fetched.

Seeking Balance

The COVID-19 pandemic has taught societies many lessons. One key takeaway is the importance of balance. While technology and control measures can be vital tools during a health crisis, they shouldn't transmute into mechanisms for societal control. As the world edges towards a new normal, it's crucial to remember the values of privacy, freedom, and autonomy and ensure they aren't casualties in the battle against future crises.

Further Reading:

1. "The Rules of Contagion: Why Things Spread - and Why They Stop" by Adam Kucharski.
2. "The Age of Surveillance Capitalism: The Fight for a Human Future at the New Frontier of Power" by Shoshana Zuboff.
3. "Viral: The Search for the Origin of COVID-19" by Alina Chan and Matt Ridley.

Chapter 9

Food and Water "The Crux of Control"

In a world rife with advanced technologies and sophisticated control mechanisms, the pillars of life—food and water—remain as fundamental as ever. History demonstrates that controlling these essentials gives unprecedented power, a lesson not lost on those aiming to guide society's course. As we gaze into the 21st century's intricate maze of geopolitics, corporate strategies, and silent wars, a striking theme emerges: our most basic needs are becoming central to an elaborate, multifaceted control mechanism.

The Ancient Strategy: Greece to Modern Eras

Historians often recount how ancient civilizations like the Greeks understood the strategic value of controlling food and water supplies. Seizing granaries and aqueducts could determine the outcome of wars. Fast forward to today, and this strategy, albeit more sophisticated and covert, continues to influence global power dynamics.

The Modern Tactic: Corporate Dominance

In the modern world, the battleground isn't just vast fields or water sources; it's in boardrooms and stock exchanges. Companies like Monsanto, with its near-monopoly over seeds and genetically modified crops, play pivotal roles in determining global food security. These conglomerates wield more than just economic power; they guide policies, influence research, and, most crucially, control a significant portion of the world's food supply.

Meanwhile, magnates like Bill Gates are investing heavily in water sources, a move some critics interpret as a bid for "blue gold" supremacy. As freshwater becomes scarcer, owning and controlling these resources becomes synonymous with wielding power.

The Double-Edged Sword: Technological Advancements

Technological strides in agriculture—be it drought-resistant crops or precision farming—promise to alleviate some challenges posed by "climate change" and rising global food demands. However, these advancements also come with concerns. Dependence on a handful of tech-savvy corporations for seeds, farming equipment, and technology potentially places enormous power in a few hands.

Poisoning the Well: Chemicals and Our Health

As if the corporate stranglehold wasn't concerning enough, there's the issue of what's in our food and water. Excessive fertilizers, pesticides, and novel chemicals taint crops, while water sources in various regions suffer contamination from substances like silver iodide and fluoride. While some argue these additions are for the greater good—improving crop yield or dental health—others highlight potential long-term health repercussions and further dependence on external entities for 'clean' alternatives.

Agenda 23 and Smart Cities: The Future Blueprint

Agenda 23, often viewed as a successor to the Agenda 21 sustainability plan, places significant emphasis on "Smart Cities." These urban centers, characterized by state-of-the-art tech infrastructure, promise efficient, sustainable living. However, beneath this glossy exterior lies a blueprint for unprecedented control.

In a smart city, everything—from the water you drink to the food you consume—is monitored, tracked, and optimized using technology. Proponents argue this ensures sustainability and improved quality of life. But critics warn of the risks: when a handful of corporations or governing bodies can control essentials like food and water using technology, the potential for manipulation and dependency skyrockets.

Moreover, the narrative around Agenda 23 and smart cities seems to have evolved. Initially pitched as a solution to combat global warming, it increasingly appears as a strategy to control societies, possibly more effectively than climate-centric agendas ever could.

Conclusion: The Way Forward

Recognizing these silent machinations is the first step. As global citizens, the onus is on us to remain informed, question the status quo, and champion transparency. Food and water have sustained humanity for millennia. As we advance, it's crucial these essentials remain symbols of life and nourishment, not tools of control.

Further Reading:

1. "Blue Gold: The Fight to Stop the Corporate Theft of the World's Water" by Maude Barlow and Tony Clarke.
2. "The Omnivore's Dilemma: A Natural History of Four Meals" by Michael Pollan.
3. "Smart Cities: Big Data, Civic Hackers, and the Quest for a New Utopia" by Anthony M. Townsend.
4. "Seeds of Deception: Exposing Industry and Government Lies About the Safety of the Genetically Engineered Foods You're Eating" by Jeffrey M. Smith.

Chapter 10

The Media Mirage - Unmasking the Illusion of Unbiased News

As you journey through the layers of this silent war, one question stands out: Who can you trust? The media, historically the "Fourth Estate" holding power accountable, increasingly seems compromised. The reason isn't hard to fathom; a majority of media houses in the United States are owned by just a few corporations. As of my last update in September 2021, giants like Comcast, Disney, and News Corp wield immense power over the narrative.

It's an alarming scenario, especially in a society that prizes free speech and a free press. This consolidation of media ownership has led to an overwhelming homogeneity in news reporting and an undermining of independent journalism. The Revolutionary War was fought on ideals such as liberty and free speech, yet today, an invisible war is being waged on these very tenets.

This concentration of media power has other subtle consequences. It becomes a tool of social control, molding public opinion according to corporate or political interests rather than objective truth. It can fuel the flames of division and distract from real issues, including those discussed in this book.

Further Reading:

- "Manufacturing Consent: The Political Economy of the Mass Media" by Edward S. Herman and Noam Chomsky
- "The Death of Truth: Notes on Falsehood in the Age of Trump" by Michiko Kakutani

So, how do we fight this media monopoly and reclaim the spirit of unbiased journalism? The first step is awareness. By recognizing the limits of mainstream media, we can begin to seek alternative, independent sources. The internet has democratized information; let's use it to break the chains of media manipulation.

This chapter is not a call to distrust every media outlet but an invitation to be discerning consumers of news. As citizens of the world, it is our duty to hold power accountable, to be the patriots our forefathers imagined when they envisioned a land of the free.

Now that we've unmasked the media's role in this silent war, are you ready to discover what you can do to make a difference?

Chapter 11

What You Can Do - Taking Back Control in the Silent War

If you've come this far, you've navigated the minefield of misinformation, glimpsed the dark underbelly of corporate monopolies, and recognized the subtle yet pervasive ways in which our world is changing. So, what can you do? How can we collectively turn the tide in this silent war?

Be Informed

Awareness is the first step toward change. Continue to seek unbiased, reliable sources of information. Don't settle for one side of the story—expose yourself to multiple perspectives, even those you disagree with.

Engage in Dialogue

Open dialogue fosters understanding. Engage with those who hold differing viewpoints. In a world trying to divide us, **understanding** is the first step toward unity. Remember, the Revolutionary War wasn't just fought with bullets and cannons; it was fought with words, ideas, and impassioned speeches about freedom and human rights.

Vote with Your Wallet

Be mindful of where you spend your money. Supporting ethical businesses can help shift the balance of power away from the corporations manipulating our world.

Community Involvement

Involvement starts at the community level. Whether it's attending town meetings, participating in local projects, or simply getting to know your neighbors, every action counts.

Further Reading:

- "The Activist's Handbook" by Randy Shaw
- "This is an Uprising" by Mark Engler and Paul Engler

Be a Beacon of Love

Ultimately, we can conquer only with love, the most potent weapon. Martin Luther King Jr. reminded us that "darkness cannot drive out darkness; only light can do that. Hate cannot drive out hate; only love can do that."

This silent war may be unlike any conflict we've faced, but it doesn't mean we're powerless. Each one of us has a role to play. Each one of us can be a soldier in this war, armed not with weapons of destruction but with love, truth, and the indomitable spirit that has defined humanity at its best.

This book aims to empower you with knowledge, but the next step is yours to take. Will you be a spectator, or will you join the ranks of those fighting for a better world? Choose wisely, for the future may depend on it.

Advocate for Policy Change

Lobby for policies that promote transparency, accountability, and sustainable practices. Don't underestimate the impact of collective voices pressing for change. Utilize online platforms to raise awareness and organize community actions.

Foster Education

In an age where misinformation is rampant, education is more important than ever. Encourage young people to question, analyze, and think critically about the world around them. A well-educated populace is harder to deceive and manipulate.

Mental and Emotional Resilience

Equip yourself with mental and emotional tools to navigate the challenges ahead. Books, workshops, and courses on resilience can help you adapt and remain stable, even when facing the complexities of modern life.

Be Prepared

It's wise to prepare for emergencies. Keep essentials like food, water, and medicines. However, remember that hoarding contributes to scarcity and panic. Be sensible and community-oriented in your preparations.

Further Reading:

- "The Art of Happiness" by Dalai Lama
- "Deep Adaptation" by Jem Bendell

Ending Note: The Call to Arms is a Call to Hearts

As you close this book, remember that you're not alone. Countless people are waking up to the realities described here, realizing the scope of what we term as the silent war of our times. This isn't a call to arms in the way you might think. No shots need be fired, only vaccines distributed, and fires quelled.

The Revolutionary War was fought to secure freedoms that today are subtly but certainly being eroded. Much like how the boiling frog doesn't realize it's in hot water until it's too late, we may not recognize the gravity of our situation until our freedoms have evaporated. But unlike that frog, we have the means to jump out of the water, to turn down the heat.

The fight for our future, for our freedoms, and for our very humanity is upon us. But remember, in the wise words of Abraham Lincoln, "With malice toward none; with charity for all." Let us strive on to do our duty and reveal the better angels of our nature.

Our united stand, our collective awakening, is the only way forward. This book is but a guide, a tool in your arsenal, but the true power for change lies within you, "We the people". Love is the key. NSIII

Thank you for joining me on this journey. The next chapter is yours to write...

Resources

On Disaster Capitalism

1. "The Shock Doctrine" by Naomi Klein
2. "Disaster Capitalism: Making a Killing out of Catastrophe" by Antony Loewenstein

On Climate Change and Environmental Impact

1. "Silent Spring" by Rachel Carson
2. "This Changes Everything: Capitalism vs. The Climate" by Naomi Klein

On Media Influence and Bias

1. "Manufacturing Consent: The Political Economy of the Mass Media" by Edward S. Herman and Noam Chomsky
2. "Trust Me, I'm Lying: Confessions of a Media Manipulator" by Ryan Holiday

On Technological Influence and Control

1. "The Age of Surveillance Capitalism" by Shoshana Zuboff
2. "Future Crimes" by Marc Goodman

On Mental and Emotional Resilience

1. "The Art of Happiness" by Dalai Lama
2. "Deep Adaptation" by Jem Bendell

On Food Security and Agriculture

1. "The Omnivore's Dilemma" by Michael Pollan
2. "Stuffed and Starved: The Hidden Battle for the World Food System" by Raj Patel

On Government Oversight and Accountability

1. "The Fifth Risk" by Michael Lewis
2. "Dark Money: The Hidden History of the Billionaires Behind the Rise of the Radical Right" by Jane Mayer

On Public Health and Vaccination

1. "On Immunity: An Inoculation" by Eula Biss
2. "The Vaccine Race: Science, Politics, and the Human Costs of Defeating Disease" by Meredith Wadman

On Homelessness and Social Issues

1. "Evicted: Poverty and Profit in the American City" by Matthew Desmond
2. "The Color of Law: A Forgotten History of How Our Government Segregated America" by Richard Rothstein

Websites and Online Tools

1. OpenSecrets.org[1] - To follow the money in politics.
2. Snopes[2] - For debunking misinformation.
3. The Bureau of Investigative Journalism[3] - For deep-dive, accountable reporting.

Please note that the listing of these resources does not imply an endorsement of all the views contained within them. They are provided to inspire further investigation and thought.

---

1. https://www.opensecrets.org/

2. https://www.snopes.com/

3. https://www.thebureauinvestigates.com/

Don't miss out!

Visit the website below and you can sign up to receive emails whenever Nicholas Salerno III publishes a new book. There's no charge and no obligation.

https://books2read.com/r/B-A-KCMK-WOZNC

BOOKS 2 READ

Connecting independent readers to independent writers.

Did you love *WW3 Isn't What You Thought It Would Be*? Then you should read *The Battle Plan Against Addiction*[4] by Nicholas Salerno III!

[5]

The Battle Plan Against Addiction

Actively help a friend, family member, or loved one fight the battle of addiction. Understanding the addict and addiction. Your role in all this, and reconnecting back to self. Putting together an intervention and getting them the help they need. Coaching, and further assistance. Lots of resources and links to further education on all topics discussed, and much more.

By Nicholas Salerno III

---

4. https://books2read.com/u/31l7Pa

5. https://books2read.com/u/31l7Pa

Also by Nicholas Salerno III

Dude Smith
The Adventures of Dude Smith

PULP Comic
Lady On The Road
The Wanderer (comic/manga)

Robot Girl
Robot Girl "Escape to Paradise"

The fantastic dog adventures of Kudo
The Greatest Dog In The World
Superhero Dog And Friends
The Fantastic dog adventures Of Kudo

The Wanderer
The Wanderer, Saving Paradise

About the Author

Nicholas Salerno III is an author, certified coach, painter, and app creator. He has authored four books including two novels as well as a biography, and his work has been published in magazines such as Martha Stewart Weddings and Sunset. He has been featured on reality television shows including Rustic Rehab, and has worked with the producers of Everybody Loves Raymond to help produce the popular reality show Extreme Makeover. **Nicholas traveled through Southeast Asia in search of traditianal natural medicines, and a better understanding of the mysterious Qi power.**

Nicholas considers himself a 'multipotentialite' - someone who has many different creative interests and pursuits. Having grown up in Oceanside, California, Nicholas grew up at the beach and is an avid surfer. One of his primary life-long interests is karate and self-defense, and he had the honor of training under Dragan Marjanovic in Hanakido karate. Dragan is a recognized master, whose sensei was Master Han, who played Billy Jack. Nicholas has his black belt in karate. Nicholas's creative pursuits include his work as a painting contractor, video making, and music. He's a skilled musician, proficient on guitar, bass, drums, and - his favorite - the native Navajo flute. He also enjoys performing as a magician.

In addition to his personal interests and pursuits, Nicholas is committed to making the world around him a better place. He served as the president of the historical Honey Run Covered Bridge in his hometown, and he has worked on many environmental projects, including an engine assist to increase fuel efficiency.

Nicholas currently resides in Northern California with his family, including his wife, Angela, and his young children, Elsa and Nico. He coaches at Up Lift a Life (upliftalife.com), his Karate style is Hanakido (*Hana* "one", *Ki* "spirit", *Do* "way"), and he developed the **"Qi Clock app"** through his app company appstacom.com, available for android and Ios.

Read more at upliftalife.com.